Awesome Activities To Help Reluctant Writers Succeed!

By Perdita Finn

SCHOLASTIC
PROFESSIONAL BOOKS

New York • Toronto • London • Auckland • Sydney
Mexico City • New Delhi • Hong Kong

Dedication

Eddie, Sherenie, Paul, Germaine, Anna and the rest of you.
Your struggles and persistence taught me so much
about writing. Thank you. This book is for you,
even though you are no longer reluctant writers.

Acknowledgements

I have been lucky in the writing teachers I have had: Lucy Calkins,
Marge Boyle, and Dorothy Barnhouse of the Teachers College Writing
Project, Natalie Goldberg, who's *Writing Down the Bones*, is such a great
invitation to reluctant writers, and Clark Strand, my husband, who
taught me what it means to have a daily writing practice
and has supported me in so many, many ways.

Cover design by Jaime Lucero
Interior design by Sydney Wright

ISBN 0-439-04389-1

Table of Contents

Introduction

The Blank Page

What Keeps Students from Writing

A blank sheet of paper can be very scary. "What am I going to write about?" we ask. "How am I going to say it? Who cares?" There isn't a writer I know who doesn't sit down each day with a certain amount of resistance. I used to think that real writers couldn't wait to start scribbling out their novels, never procrastinated, never had to trick themselves into getting started. But the more I learned about other writers and about my own writing, the more I realized that reluctance is a natural part of the writing process.

Most writers manage to push through their initial hesitations. They have little rituals that help them get started on their daily work—a walk, a cup of tea, a little reading. The French novelist Colette used to pick all the fleas off her cat before opening her journal each day, and Toni Morrison has said that she begins by giving herself permission to write badly. She knows that what's most difficult is not writing well but just beginning to write at all.

We need some experience with the writing process, however, before we can trust it—trust that one sentence will lead to another, trust that we don't have to know where we're headed when we begin, trust that, yes, finally, we can create something that other people will enjoy reading. When we finally adopt a daily writing practice, the very ordinariness of it will carry us through most of our writing anxieties. But many students, unfortunately, never make it beyond their initial reluctance; they have no positive experiences with the writing process, so when faced with a blank sheet of paper, they are paralyzed.

Some reluctant writers lack basic skills: They've never read much, they still have lots of trouble with simple spelling and punctuation, and they have limited vocabularies. Frequently, they are terrified to begin because they don't want to reveal how inadequate their writing is. Their only experience of writing is of failure. These students need lots of confidence building. They need to become familiar with the writing process through genres that are accessible to them, to learn to say simple things well, and to feel some success with their ability to use words. Once they are more comfortable with writing and writing every day, their skills will begin to improve.

Others seem to be capable enough but will nevertheless only scribble a few words in their notebooks or fail to turn in writing assignments. Frequently, these students are anxious about the amount of self-revelation that writing can demand. When asked to write about what they know best, their concern is that they will have to write about who they are, and for many different reasons—cultural, psychological, personal—they don't want to. It's true that the writing-workshop classroom, with its emphasis on poetry, memoir, and personal essays, has been liberating for many students, but it can actually be inhibiting to others.

In order to find their voice, these more-inhibited students need instead to work with genres that allow them some protective distance. Ultimately, as they feel more comfortable, they may even begin to experiment with a wider range of forms. The activities in this book are focused around genres that are both easily accessible to students and demand less-personal exploration.

The activities in Chapter 1, The Writer's Notebook, are designed to encourage students' writing fluency and help them over the stumbling blocks of getting started, finding things to write about, and letting thoughts and ideas flow. In Chapter 2, a study of advertising allows students to examine the persuasive language with which they are most familiar and, as they create their own successful ad campaign, learn the different ways they can play with words. In Chapter 3, a study of picture books will allow even the least-skilled students to become quickly familiar with many different authors and styles of writing and to create an actual book that friends and siblings can delight in. When they write mysteries (Chapter 4), they can, in the midst of sequencing and hiding clues, engage in traditional outlining activities in an untraditional way. Finally, with sports journalism (Chapter 5), students can build on their often already extensive knowledge of teams and players as they produce a classroom magazine. Each section breaks the writing project into easy-to-do

activities that won't intimidate students—bringing students to the writing process in small, manageable steps.

In deciding which activities and genre studies to focus on with your own class, it is important to consider your students' skills, interests, and concerns. The objective is to provide reluctant writers with an entry point into the writing process that will feel safe and familiar to them.

In order to help reluctant writers, we first have to remove all of their concerns and inhibitions except one—getting started. Good writing takes us in unexpected directions and, like any journey into the unknown, it can be frightening not knowing what we will discover along the way. Occasionally, those students who are most reluctant to write are fully aware of how powerful words can be. Unlike the students who are less engaged with meanings and language, they are actually justified in their awe of what they might say.

Once I taught a girl who would literally barely touch her pencil to the page. Her cramped, almost-invisible markings rarely said more than, "I got new sneakers yesterday," or, "I hate that girl." She kept herself slumped over in her chair and almost never talked to me. Until we started a unit on picture books. Until she read Lucille Clifton's *Three Wishes*. Then she began working steadily on elaborate drawings of a little girl holding a teddy bear. She began to write words under the pictures in pencil and to finally go over the pencil with black ink. "Platrea's Fall," the story she wrote and illustrated, was a sad and deeply moving fantasy about a little girl's disappearance after a fight with her mother. We all loved her book, and she was proud of it. It would be a long time before she would write about her own mother who was dying of AIDS or the foster family she lived with, but it took only one successful experience of the writing process to overcome her reluctance for writing itself. After that one project, she called herself a writer, read a speech she wrote for the whole school, and always wrote in pen.

However we help our students gain entry into the writing process, we must never forget how exhilarating it can feel to experience success. Ultimately, it is that memory that encourages us when we feel reluctant and unable to begin. "All right, I can do this," we say to ourselves and pick up our pen.

Chapter 1

The Writer's Notebook

Encouraging Fluency

Reluctant writers are often overly concerned with the mechanics of writing. They tend to be anxious about spelling, punctuation, and handwriting. They cross out and erase, they stop to look up words in the dictionary, they crumple up innumerable sheets of paper. Often they just sit there waiting for the perfect words to appear out of the air. What inhibits them is the belief that it has to be correct the first time. It doesn't.

Writing is a process of approximation. Usually, we don't even know what we want to write about until we're halfway through our journal. We ramble on and on until we finally discover our real questions and ideas. Then we write more. Then we cut and shape and twist until we get what we want. Eventually, we ask for help in editing our piece and then we copyedit—often with lots of help.

The writer's notebook is a place for the student to experiment and to begin to enjoy language and the creation of writing. All writers keep some kind of notebook or journal. And these are invariably filled with scribbled sentences, half-baked ideas, complaints, musings, and sometimes the seed of a story or a poem.

For the reluctant writer, what's most important is that we remove all restrictions but one—writing itself. "Nothing matters," I tell my students, "but that you *do* it." I set the timer and we write—*anything*—for ten minutes. "I don't know what to write!" shouts one student. "Okay," I say. "Write that." "I hate this!" yells another. "Great! Write about it!" Eventually, when students are writing every day, when they are producing pieces and are confident about what they have to say, they can become concerned again with mechanics. First, however, they must write.

Blabber (or, Don't Think, Just Write!)

Everyone has a thousand and one thoughts passing through his or her mind at any moment. "What's for lunch today? Look at David's cool pen! My foot's asleep. What's the teacher saying? I can't wait to get out of here and play soccer. . . ." All we have to do as writers is grab onto one of those thoughts and hang on for the ride. We might start writing about lunch or soccer and then go on to describe our dog or last night's dinner, and before we know it, ten minutes are up. No one's mind is empty. The challenge is just to write down whatever's passing through, without deciding if it's important, interesting, boring, or stupid. Just as we let thoughts pass easily through our head, we have to let them pass through our hand to our writer's notebook.

THE ACTIVITY

1. To help students begin to develop a concentrated writing practice, begin by offering the following guidelines:

   ◆ **No stopping.** Even if you have to write "I don't know what to write about," you have to keep writing. You are training your hand and your mind.

   ◆ **Spelling, punctuation, grammar, and handwriting don't count.** You need to be able to read it back to yourself, but that's all. Certainly don't stop to look up words or ask for help or worry about anything.

   ◆ **Write sentences and not just words or, in other words, write whole thoughts and not just shorthand.** The goal of this practice is to eventually be able to "think" with the hand, to let the words flow directly from the brain to the pen and paper. That flow is achieved with sentences and ideas that lead into each other. If students are just noting single words— *cat, baseball, tomorrow*—they actually are editing much of what they are thinking and so stopping the flow. The goal is to capture everything.

- **Don't think, just write**. Really, this means don't plan ahead and don't criticize or judge yourself or your writing as you write. Write down whatever comes along—good, bad, indifferent.

2. Next, if you dare, give students a live demonstration of a teacher blabbering. I assign one student to be the timekeeper (three minutes is usually enough to get the point across) and ask another to give me a topic, any topic. Then I grab my chalk, head to the board, and I'm off. "Write about cats," shouts one of the kids and I scribble:

   My daughter wants a kitten or a Pomeranian. A Pomeranian is one of those horrible yappy dogs that has sharp little teeth. I got her a stuffed one for Christmas because one day at the park this lady let her walk her Pomeranian called Tyrone and she fell in love with it because it was actually little enough for her to walk. Our cats would eat a Pomeranian I'm sure of it. I'd like to eat lunch now. I've got a great tomato sandwich. I've eaten tomato sandwiches ever since I read Harriet the Spy . . .

3. Ask students to tell you what they noticed about blabbering while you were doing it. They will probably notice that you misspelled words, that your handwriting was horrible, that you didn't even write about the topic, that you switched topics. (I sometimes deliberately accentuate these things in my own demonstration.) Point out to them that all that matters is that you didn't stop.

4. Now it's their turn! Set the timer for five minutes. Whenever you see a student stop, nudge him or her back to writing. Sometimes I even point out what a good workout writing can be! Kids are often very tired after really writing nonstop for five minutes.

5. Try to work for up to ten minutes, and then fifteen.

6. For homework, ask them to do two five-minute blabbers. (Or more if they are up to it!)

Entry Points

While we can write about anything in our writer's notebook, it can be helpful sometimes to assign ourselves a particular place to start— especially if we find that we freeze up when we look at that blank piece of paper.

What's important is knowing that *we don't have to stick with the topic we give ourselves*. It's just a way of loosening ourselves up so we can find out what we really want to say. The topic is only an entry point, and there is no way of predicting what we'll write about once the door is open. Inexperienced writers often believe that they must find their focus right away. Then, when they don't, they feel like they have nothing to say. More-experienced writers know they can write all over the place and then find their focus later on, during the revision process.

THE ACTIVITY ♢◆ ♢◆ ♢◆ ♢◆ ♢◆ ♢◆ ♢◆ ♢◆

1. Have students fill out the Entry Points activity sheet (page 16), generating a list of possible entry points. It may be important to remind students that these are not topics they are going to be stuck with no matter what, but are just subjects they know about. They're more like jumper cables when the car won't start.

2. While students are filling out their sheets, I like to walk around and point out topics I know they love. "Don't forget to put 'dirt bikes' on your list," I'll say to one, or "Did you remember to write *Star Wars*?" I encourage students to trust their real interests.

3. After students have generated their lists, they can try choosing one of the entry points and using it as a starting place for their free writing. Have students try a couple of different entry points and see which ones are more productive. Which ones allow them to write for the longest time? There are certain entry points, students will discover, that they return to again and again, that always get them started on their writing.

4. Students should keep their entry-point lists in their notebooks and add to them as new interests arise.

Stop Making Sense

Inspiration. Where does it come from? In a certain sense, nobody really knows; but any writer who has experienced it will say that suddenly she felt that the words were just flowing onto the paper or, as the classic poets used to put it, that the muse had taken over.

Certainly it involves an ability to open ourselves up to whatever ideas are inside of us and to trust where those ideas may lead us. Often writers who are stuck or at a loss for words are trying to make the writing happen, to control it, to figure it all out ahead of time. A real challenge for reluctant writers is to give up that need for control and to let what happens happen. I often tell my students that their brains are like icebergs—the visible tip is not very interesting but what lies beneath the surface is large and powerful. Sometimes these students just need to stop trying so hard, to relax and have fun, and to let themselves be surprised by what they come up with. Often when we stop trying to make sense, different, more meaningful ideas and thoughts emerge.

THE ACTIVITY

1. To loosen students up, try playing the following concentration game, the objective of which is to see which student can talk for the most time on a trivial topic. It doesn't matter what the players say—how silly, ridiculous, or nonsensical—as long as they keep talking about the assigned topic. In fact, the topics that are chosen—dust bunnies, door handles, cat's whiskers—often encourage the players to be wacky.

   The two players sit next to each other and wait for the assigned topic (either from the teacher or another student). As soon as they hear it, they must begin talking—simultaneously. They may say whatever they want about the topic. (With some groups, of course, it may be necessary to remind them not to use obscenities.) The only rules are 1) they can't stop talking for any reason, and 2) they have to keep—very generally—on the topic. The first student to stop talking loses.

   What students will discover is that the successful players say whatever comes into their head, they follow trains of thought, and they never plan anything or worry about making sense. They make things up, they remember things, they keep on going.

"I love dust bunnies. They hop around under my bed. Hop. Hop. Hop. Making me sneeze, curling up in the corner and always around my socks. Why are there always so many dust bunnies behind doors and under beds and under couches? They are like tumbleweeds blowing across the desert. Maybe dust bunnies and tumbleweeds are related. I must say I like vacuuming them up. Swoosh. I always have to vacuum my room on Saturdays. I hate that. Maybe dust bunnies hate Saturday-morning cleaning as much as I do. Where do the dust bunnies go after I vacuum them up?"

2. Students usually enjoy this game a lot and get better at it as they play it. The next step, then, is to translate it into their writing. Who can write the most about some silly topic? The master of this, of course, is humorist Dave Barry, and after this activity students might enjoy listening to one of his pieces. Does he plan what he is going to say, or does he open himself up and let whatever thoughts come into his head land on the paper?

3. The final challenge is for students to take the same freedom and playfulness they have exercised with these silly topics to something that matters more to them. They can return to their own lists of entry points and try assigning themselves their own topics. Even the most serious topics can be handled lightly, expansively. As writers, we have to be ready to be surprised by what we might say.

Wondering

A common misconception of students is that they must know everything they want to say before they begin to write. In fact, much great writing begins with questions, so that the writing is a way of exploring possible answers. As writers, it is important to let ourselves be confused, troubled, uncertain, quizzical, and amazed. It can be such a relief to realize that, at least in writing, there is no single right answer—just many different ways of thinking about a question.

1. Have students begin by generating as many questions as possible either in groups or individually. It may be helpful to give them some starters, such as:

   What if . . .
   How come . . .
   Why . . .
   Will it ever . . .
   How is it possible . . .

   Ask students to think about things that happened in the past, are happening right now, or might happen in the future. Encourage them to be outlandish: "What if the polar ice cap really did melt?" "What if I could fly?" Then quite ordinary: "Why did I fight with my mom this morning?" "How come I love soccer so much?" Some questions may be personal, others not at all: "What if Scottie Pippen played for the Nets?"

2. These questions are now entry points for their writing in their notebooks. When students write in response to these questions, they can be encouraged to play with many possible answers: "One answer might be . . ." they can begin. "Another might be . . ."

3. Students may want to try creating a web of possible answers. They can draw a circle containing their question in the center of the page and then lines extending in all directions—each one leading to a different possible answer. And those answers don't need to be single words or sentences, but can be long paragraphs or even stories.

Undercover Agents

I always used to hesitate about confiding anything to a friend of mine who was a novelist. Invariably, some detail from my life, some conversation I'd told her about or some crazy story, would end up in one of her books—disguised, but recognizable to me.

Writers' imaginations are fueled by the ordinary stuff in the world around them—the people they meet, the scraps of conversations they overhear on the bus, the briefest stories in the newspaper. Some of what they write they invent; some, they just capture. All beginning writers need to be encouraged to notice what's happening around them more and to take that material and use it toward their own ends.

THE ACTIVITY

1. Have each student bring to class a small notebook they can easily conceal. (If necessary, they can also make them by stapling together paper.) These will be their "spy records."

2. Explain to students that they will be undercover agents listening to interesting conversations, noticing important details, describing curious individuals. You may also want to tell them that spies, and writers, are very careful not to let people know they are watching them. They must be nonchalant, but attentive.

3. For their first assignment, you may want them to listen for an interesting conversation and simply record it. They may hear it in the cafeteria, in the hallway, on the bus or the subway, or in line at the grocery store. In addition to writing down the dialogue, the students may want to record interesting things they noticed about the setting.

4. Next, take them for a walk outside or through the hallway and tell them that anything they see might be important. What do they notice that no one else notices? What small things catch their attention? They can record these in their notebook. They might be clues!

5. Another time, have them look for interesting characters. Describe their appearance, their actions, their words.

6. In class, students can have meetings in which they share what they have discovered. Eventually, they may want to use one of these observations as the starting point for a story or an essay. Let them know, however, that many writers never know exactly how they will use all the information they record until the moment occurs. Suddenly in the midst of writing about something they recall a detail or a person they noticed last week or last year that would fit perfectly. What matters is that they are always collecting material, they are always listening and noticing.

Assessing a Writer's Notebook

The objective of the writer's notebook is to loosen students up—to make them less self-critical about what they have to say, more open to the ideas they actually have, more fluent in their writing. Because of this, I do not grade students on the quality of their writing. With reluctant writers, I am more interested in the fact that they are writing at all. Therefore, I evaluate their notebooks on how much writing they have done. At this stage of the game, quantity is what counts.

Have they written for the full ten or fifteen minutes each day in class? Have they been writing in their notebooks for homework? Sometimes I will create a challenge, "Who can write the most in his or her notebook this week?" Sometimes we will have an in-class "test" where we try to write without stopping and see how long we can go!

Eventually, once students pick up their pens effortlessly and scribble words quickly across the page, I show them ways of using their notebooks to train themselves as writers—experimenting with language, perspective, and genres. With reluctant writers, however, we must not lose sight of the first steps—developing fluency and confidence.

Entry Points

1. Five things I know a lot about:

2. Five things I'm really interested in:

3. Five things I don't know anything about but I still think are cool:

4. A few things that make me angry:

5. Things that make me happy:

6. My favorite activities:

7. The people I think about the most:

8. What I'm thinking about when I look out the window during class:

9. What my friends and I like to talk about:

10. Ten things I see or experience every day:

My Writer's Notebook—A Self-Assessment

1. I have _____ full pages of writing in my notebook.

2. The longest piece of writing I have is _____ pages. I wrote for _____ minutes.

3. The thing I wrote that most surprised me is . . .

4. What I like best that I wrote is . . .

5. The longest I can write for without stopping is _____ minutes.

6. The hardest thing about writing in my notebook is . . .

7. The easiest thing about writing in my notebook is . . .

8. My goal as a writer is to . . .

Chapter 2

An Advertising Campaign

The Power of Persuasive Language

Some of the first words children read are found on billboards or in magazine ads. The language of advertising is everywhere—on TV, on the Internet, in newspapers and magazines. Just do it. Things go better with Coke. Got milk? Of all the writing genres that students study in school, the form with which they are actually most familiar is advertising copy.

The use of language in many advertisements is as sophisticated as that of any poem. Advertisers know the power of precise words—their sounds, their implied meanings, their rhythms and rhymes. Any study of advertising writing, then, has the advantage of being both very accessible and as worthy of serious study as poetry. In fact, many students who are disinterested in poetry are eager to learn the same concepts when they are studying advertising writing. They know it, and they have respect for how it works.

Yet they are not often aware of how the words in advertising work on them; children, more than others, are at the mercy of advertising, first wanting this toy or breakfast cereal they see on TV, then this pair of sneakers or that brand of jeans. Studying advertising, learning how ad copy works and how to write it, helps to make children aware of the techniques being used and thus less susceptible to manipulation. Perhaps no other unit of study more clearly reveals how powerful words can be.

Developing a Product

Just what we need—another bottled water, gourmet ice cream, perfume, high-priced sneaker! Yet somehow, with clever marketing, advertisers are able to convince us that this is the product we've been looking for all our lives, the very thing that will make us healthier, happier, and wiser. How do they do it?

One of the first steps in creating a new product is deciding what to call it. The very name of something can grab our interest or cause us to turn away. When a company wanted to sell a new, high-quality brand of ice cream, they decided to call it Häagen-Dazs. Everyone assumed it must be Danish and thus made with Old World care; and, moreover, if it was imported, most people would be willing to pay more. In fact, it was made in America, and the name was invented just so people would assume it was imported and therefore better.

Names matter. They carry with them meanings, associations, and feelings. When we think about what effect they have on us, we can begin to engage with the power inherent in all words.

THE ACTIVITY

1. Working in groups or as a class, students should choose one of the following products to investigate—a bottled water, a perfume, a sneaker, an ice cream, or a laundry detergent. Then they should make a list of all the different brands currently available and their names. They may want to look through magazines, watch television for homework, or just use their own, usually quite extensive, knowledge.

2. Next, students should think about what feelings each of the names gives them. It may be helpful to explain to students the difference between the denotation, or literal meaning, of words, and the connotation, or associative meaning. For instance, Air Jordans refers to the air and Michael Jordan; the feeling, however, is that if you wear them you will fly. Jumping Michaels might not have sold so well. Why not?

3. After students have discussed the effects of product names, they can try to create a name for a new brand of perfume or sneaker or detergent. What will they call it and why? Encourage students to brainstorm a list of names and then choose the one or two they like the most. Also, just as collaboration encourages creativity in real-life advertising agencies, it may be useful for the students to work in groups.

4. When students have a name for their new brand, they can conduct some market research to determine its effectiveness. They should tell the rest of the class the name and ask what associations and feelings the name has for them. Is the name appealing? Why or why not? They may want to try out two or three different names in order to find out which one is most effective.

Persuasions

Advertisers are not just providing us with information about a product; they are trying to convince us to buy their brand instead of any other. Often we have no real need for what they are trying to sell us (our own tap water is just as tasty and as safe as most bottled water, it turns out), but it is the advertisers' job to convince us otherwise—that our lives will be better if we buy their brand.

Some messages are explicit—they give us specific reasons why a product is better than any other: "Free." "Better than ever." "New and improved." And some messages are implicit—they imply that our lives will be happier if we put on this perfume or drink that brand of soda. What makes their product the best? That is the question the advertiser is always trying to answer.

THE ACTIVITY

1. Choose a popular advertisement for students to study. Ask students to consider what the ad is promising the reader. What are the explicit advantages of using the product? What are the implicit advantages?

2. Now have students think about the brand they named in the earlier activity. Why is their product better than all the others? What reasons can they invent? What kinds of subtle promises would they like to make about their product? Have students brainstorm a list of reasons both reasonable and ridiculous.

3. One way that advertisers convey implicit messages is with pictures. At this point in their advertising campaign, students may want to create illustrations to get their point across. Reluctant writers often find writing easier when they can derive inspiration from their drawing.

Identifying a Target Audience

Advertisers need to think carefully about their audience before they begin writing copy. Who's going to be reading this? What are their interests, concerns, and questions, and how can we take them into consideration? The celebrities used in the Got milk? ads vary with the targeted audience. In *Sports Illustrated*, it's Mark McGwire with a milk mustache; in *Ladies Home Journal*, it's Melanie Griffith surrounded by her children. Learning how to shape material for a particular audience is an important skill for all writers. For the advertiser trying to sell a product, it is essential.

THE ACTIVITY

1. Bring in a variety of magazines for children to study. These can be collected from libraries or brought from home. What kind of products are advertised in *Family Circle*, in *Teen People*, in *Time*, in *Sports Illustrated*? In what ways do the advertisers appeal to these different audiences? (Students may notice that the pictures used are different, the language is different, etc.)

2. Advertisers are very precise about their target audiences (i.e., unmarried women between the ages of 22 and 28 or boys between 9 and 12). Cut out some ads

from various magazines. Then have students see if they can figure out who the target audience is by using the Identifying a Target Audience activity sheet (page 27).

3. Ask students to choose a product and try marketing it to two different audiences. For instance, how would they try to sell sneakers to mature athletes and young kids. What pictures and images would they use? What words and slogans?

4. You may want to point out that advertisers personalize advertisements by speaking directly to their target audience, saying "you" frequently in the copy.

Warming Up with Wordplay

One of the most important ways in which advertisers catch their audiences' attention is with clever or humorous language. An ad for diapers once showed a rear view of a baby with the copy, "To be a great parent, you've got to start at the bottom." We laugh and we look more carefully. We laugh and we remember.

Words are fun, and there are all kinds of ways we can play with them. For reluctant writers, however, words are often the enemy. To help them loosen their grip on language, set aside time to just play with words—to make associations, to explore their possible meanings, to enjoy their sounds and rhythms. Many of the following ideas are used by ad writers as they sit around a table tossing back and forth all kinds of words and ideas.

THE ACTIVITY

1. Free association is a technique is which we let a word or idea trigger another word or idea in our head. Often the connection between the original word and the one it triggers is neither obvious nor logical—and yet something about it may make a subtle kind of sense. Psychologists, of course, have used this technique for a long time to help people discover their hidden feelings. Writers, though, use it to free up their thinking, to open their imaginations to new possibilities.

To help students learn how to free-associate, begin by saying a word and then having the students write down the first word that comes into their head. "Dog," says the teacher. "Cat," writes one student. "Bones," writes another.

Expand the exercise by having the students use the word they write down as a trigger for a new association—they can even follow one word to another in a chain. For instance the teacher says, "Lunch" and a student might write:

> *peanut butter, sticky, honey, Pooh Bear, my little brother, diapers,*
> *bad smells, the dump, seagulls, flying, clouds, winds*

Note that the only person who needs to understand the association between one word and another is the writer, although when sharing their lists students may want to explain their connections.

2. Webbing, a technique with which many teachers are already familiar, is much like free association, only we are continually returning to the original word for new inspiration. Students can try a practice web using a simple subject like school or cars and then can try doing a web based on their advertising product. Webs that employ free association can be very expansive and playful.

3. After students have collected lots of different words associated with their product, they can try mixing them up in different combinations to create interesting headlines and slogans. For instance, a recent oatmeal ad reads, "Like a hug that lasts all day." That writer free-associated from breakfast to Mom to that kiss good-bye at the door and found a whole image for the advertisement.

4. Popular expressions and slang words or phrases can also offer students ideas for their lists. For instance, in an ad for frozen food, the copy reads, "What do you do for dinner when you'd rather be chillin' with the kids?" Chillin' is a pun on the slang word for "hanging out" and also, of course, implies the coldness of frozen food.

5. Another way for students to play with words is to experiment with oxymorons. An oxymoron is a pairing of words that are ostensibly opposites but that nevertheless reveal the truth about something. An ad for clothes that are "luxuriously

simple," or for a product called "Soft Scrub," catches our attention with its seeming contradictions. Have students take a few of the words from their webs and see if they can find their opposites. Are there any appealing or intriguing combinations?

6. Finally, encourage students to collect expressions, words, and phrases that they think are funny or cool. The more attention they begin to pay to the words they hear around them every day, the more they may begin to enjoy them.

Brevity Is the Soul of Wit

The best writing is straightforward: It uses one word instead of two, and an ordinary vocabulary. Unfortunately, inexperienced writers often associate long with good, and we shudder when they hand us their ten-page story. In fact, writers often find it much harder to be concise than verbose, and one of a writer's most important skills is knowing what to leave out.

Advertisers can't afford to be long-winded. The faster they get their message across, the more likely their audience will pay attention. A recent ad for Volkswagen's revived Bug merely said, "0-60? Yes." It didn't say, "It's the same old car you remember: not that fast, but filled with charm."

One paradox of precise language, however, is that we often need to write a lot in order to write a little. As writers, we first need to be relaxed and fluent in collecting all that we want to say. Then we need to be ruthless, crossing out everything that's not absolutely necessary.

THE ACTIVITY

1. Ask students to think about a time they were very scared and to free-write about that experience for at least ten minutes. If any students balk at this, explain to them that any time of strong emotion—happiness, sadness, embarrassment—will do.

2. Now have them count the number of words they have written and then cut out half of them. What's necessary? What's less necessary? Repeat this two or three times, until finally the students have just ten or twenty words to express their experience. What are they? How did they choose? What effect do they have?

3. For their advertisements, students should now write as much as they can about their products. What are its benefits? What might be consumers' concerns? What's so special about this item? Next, have them try cutting out most of the words. Finally, what is really necessary to say?

4. Often, as students prioritize what is most important to say, they will discover that they want to change the words they are using. This shows they are engaged with thinking about what is the best language to accurately express themselves. It shows they are becoming writers.

The Campaign: A Collaborative Writing Project

Advertisers have a very simple way of determining the success of their work—does it sell the product? Creating an advertising campaign to display in the classroom or school can be a very powerful way for students to realize how important writing is in the real world. Often, too, when their writing is not just for their teacher but for their peers, students begin to care passionately about its quality.

THE ACTIVITY

1. Divide the students into groups, each of which will be its own advertising agency. Have each agency choose a product to focus on or, if the class can tolerate the competition, the teacher may choose one product and the different agencies can compete with each other to see who can market it most successfully.

2. The campaign itself can either be conducted in the classroom or could utilize the hallways or lunchroom of the school.

3. Each group should name their product and develop at least three advertisements for it. Those ads might be related, such as the Got milk? series, or each completely different. As students work collaboratively, they should be sure to make use of one another's strengths. Who are the illustrators? the photographers? the comics?

4. Students will want to think carefully about ad placement and the frequency with which they change ads. If they change the ads too often, people may not have a chance to really notice them. Yet if they are left up too long, people may become bored. What works and why?

5. During the campaign, students may discover that their ads are not working—people don't get them or think they're stupid. If they want to succeed, they will have to come up with a new set of advertisements. Revision is a day-to-day activity in the real world.

6. Throughout the campaign, students should keep a daily journal of their agency's process. In addition, the teacher may want to have students designate a section of their journal for recording what they are beginning to notice in the advertising world around them. Students may want to jot down interesting uses of language in certain advertisements, the hidden messages they are beginning to perceive, or clever ways the advertisers catch people's attention.

7. Finally, students should survey their audience to discover which ads worked and why. In the real world, we are all graded—by the success or failure of our work. An advertiser who does sloppy work that no one notices will soon be out of a job. And one who creates thrilling campaigns that have everyone talking—and buying—will soon be driving a fancy car. In many ways, this feedback is a real-life grade. (Of course, as all artists know, sometimes great work does go unrecognized or is mis-understood, so you may not actually want the surveys to be students' only grade.)

Identifying a Target Audience

The target audience is the group or type of people that advertisers want to attract. People may be defined by their age, gender, family status, lifestyle, or interests.

1. How would you, as a member of a target audience, be described? (For example, someone might describe himself as an 11-year-old boy living in the country who plays computer games and is interested in the Civil War.)

2. Now study the available advertisements and fill in the following information for each advertisement.

Brand Name

Slogans or Words

Pictures: Describe the image on the advertisement.

Who is the target audience and how do you know this?

Chapter 3

Building Confidence

Writing and Illustrating Picture Books

In order to help reluctant writers engage with the whole of the writing process, from drafting through proofreading, I like to do a project—one that will appear to these students to be quite easy—on something they may already be familiar with—picture books.

Picture books are accessible to almost everyone. Yet the writing in these books, for all its seeming simplicity, is often quite sophisticated, and any student who actually sets about trying to write a good one will quickly learn much about good writing. Even the weakest students will be able to read lots of picture books, to study different authors and styles, to notice how these writers play with language and how they take their audience into consideration.

The conversation between pictures and words in these books is also reassuring for reluctant writers, many of whom are quite comfortable drawing or painting. Some students will find they know what the pictures will be before writing the story and that, as they perfect their drawings, they find they want to change their words. Still others will find themselves valued in the classroom for the first time as their artistic abilities are in high demand by other students.

Finally, in producing a piece of writing for children younger than themselves, reluctant writers immediately feel older and more experienced. They begin to discover that they can create a piece of writing that is genuinely valued by someone else.

Picture Book Immersion

We learn a language best when we are surrounded by it daily. Students who have been immersed in stories since they were little often find it effortless to create their own narratives and have vast vocabularies that have been acquired quite naturally. Often, reluctant writers have had very limited or unpleasant experiences with books. The more picture books they read (and the great thing about this project is that they can read a lot of them!), the more familiar they will become with the possibilities of the form and the easier they will find it to create their own.

THE ACTIVITY

1. Fill the room with quality picture books. Borrow from libraries, kindergarten and first-grade teachers, and your home collection. Ask students to bring in any picture books they loved when they were little or that their younger brothers and sisters currently enjoy. Try to make sure there will be books to satisfy the interests of all the students—adventure stories, humor, fantasy, and realistic memoirs.

2. On the first day, introduce some of the books and authors to the students and then make time for them to browse and read. They may want to share with the class any favorites they remember from when they were little. It may be important to remind students that they are reading these books because they are going to write one for children younger than themselves, and they are researching the genre.

3. In order to help students reflect on the books they've read, have them complete the Picture Book Response (page 38) when they are finished.

4. Throughout your study of picture books, you will want students to keep expanding their knowledge of the genre. You may want to begin each day by having a student share one of his favorite books and explain what he likes about the story and the writing. You may also want students to do a more extensive study of a favorite author.

Prewriting

When writers finally sit down to compose an essay or a story, they have often already done much of the work in their notebooks. Their casual scribblings can be shaped for an audience. It is important, then, that long before students begin to worry about what to write about, their notebooks should be filled with the seeds for stories—sentences about when they were little, lists of interests or ideas, fragments that they can build on and develop. When it actually comes time to write a story, they will discover that a lot of the work is already done.

THE ACTIVITY

1. Before students begin writing in preparation for their picture book, it may be helpful to just talk for a while about when they were little. What were they like? What were their interests? their memories? What was it like to be four or five?

2. Students can then answer the questions from the Prewriting Activity Sheet (page 39) in their notebooks. It may be helpful for them to do it in groups and share when they are done. Often, someone else's idea will trigger one of our own.

3. Using one of the answers from the sheet, students might try quickly writing a short story for a picture book. Encourage them to do it in ten minutes and not to think about it too much. When we think, we begin to worry and judge. Sometimes sheer speed can help us blast through our anxiety.

Getting to Know Your Audience

One of the most fun and useful parts of this project is having students familiarize themselves with their audience—three- to six-year olds. It may be enough to interview siblings and cousins, or the class may want to establish a relationship with a local preschool or kindergarten. Students might want to read stories to these younger children and find out what they are like. Later they can return and share with them the picture books they have written themselves.

THE ACTIVITY

1. Students may want to prepare for the interview by interviewing each other first. They can share ideas together about how best to ask questions, record the answers, and put the person they are interviewing at ease. Students can use the following questions for their interviews.

   1. *What are some of your favorite things?*
   2. *What are your favorite toys? What games do you like to play?*
   3. *Who are you friends and your favorite people?*
   4. *What are some of your wishes?*
   5. *What don't you like?*
   6. *What are some things you are scared of?*
   7. *What's the best thing that ever happened to you?*
   8. *Do you have a favorite book? What is it? What do you like about it?*
   9. *What kind of stories don't you like?*
   10. *What would you like me to tell you a story about?*
   11. *Can you tell me a story?*

2. If the class is not going to be connecting with a younger group of children, students should plan on who they are going to interview and where and when.

3. Students will want to share their results with each other when they are finished talking with the younger children. They may have discovered similar kinds of things that they will want to make use of when writing their own picture book. (Many children hate scary stories, for instance, or love books about trains or princesses.)

4. After conducting an interview, they can again try dashing out another story for a picture book inspired by something heard or thought about during the interview.

Mixing Up the Ingredients of a Story

Whenever I have to amuse a group of little kids on the spot, I ask that each of them to give me the name of one thing they want to be in a story—"A cheetah!" "A fire truck!" "Golden slippers!"—and then without a moment's hesitation, I begin. "Now most fire trucks have Dalmatians riding on the back of them, but not Jack's fire truck—no, he had a cheetah . . ." I let myself be silly, ridiculous, whatever—just so long as I use all of the children's ideas before the end. After doing this exercise a few times, of course, the kids want to be the storytellers and end up entertaining each other with similar fantastical tales.

The goal of this activity is to help students realize that creating a story is no big deal. We can do it on the spot, with whatever ingredients are available. We can churn out five or six stories in a morning and then keep only the one we like the best. Robert Munsch, the popular and prolific picture-book writer, began his career by telling stories to his preschoolers, and he has continued to get ideas from his daily storytelling. After this activity, students might enjoy reading some of his books.

THE ACTIVITY

1. Demonstrate the game to students by asking three or four of them to name an object you will include in your story. If you feel ambitious, you can ask the whole class to name something!

2. Then have students break up into groups and play together, with one person telling the story using characters or things the other people in the group have named.

3. Now students can pick two or three things from their prewriting sheets and their interviews and try quickly writing a story in their notebook. The emphasis, of course, is on playfulness, not on creating a work of art. Therefore, it can be very helpful to have them finish one and, without even a pause, try another. Encourage students to make up as many quick stories as possible.

Animals Everywhere

From Beatrix Potter to Eric Carle, picture-book writers know just how much kids love animals and stories about them. Beatrix Potter would spend hours observing and sketching the animals in the English countryside and managed in her stories to capture their exact habits and characteristics as well as certain truths about childhood itself. With his hungry caterpillars and searching hermit crabs, Eric Carle offers early science lessons and also reassuring wisdom for young readers.

For the reluctant writer, writing about animals can be easier than writing about themselves. Suddenly, for the first time, these students can write about feelings that had felt too intimate to express before. "I think Coconut is feeling a little sad," my daughter said the other day about her cat who was sitting by the window licking his paws. I put down my pen and went over to spend time with her.

THE ACTIVITY

1. Bring in a lot of different pictures of animals. You can cut them out from *National Geographic*, catalogs, or old calendars. I like to glue each picture to a piece of construction paper so that it can be used again and again.

2. Allow the students to look at the animals and choose one they really like. Have them come up with a name for this animal. Where does it live? How old is it? What does it like to do? What is it afraid of? Does it have any problems? Some students may be very literal and you will want to explain to them about anthropomorphism, or giving animals human characteristics or situations. Certainly they will understand this idea better if they have already read a lot of picture books with animal characters.

3. Ask students to make a list of common fears or problems of early childhood. How would their animal respond to such fears or problems? What would happen? Some students may want to do a series of drawings about their animal, still others might want to dramatize the situation. Eventually all of them should write a story or two about their animal.

4. Ask students to watch an animal in its natural habitat, like Beatrix Potter did. If students don't have access to family pets or a local zoo, remember there are always pigeons, squirrels and, yes, even cockroaches! Students can sketch their animal and write a description. Students can also try writing a quick story they imagined about the animal while they were observing it.

Finding the Music of Words

Because young children are just discovering language, they often take delight in the sheer sound of words. They'll find a word they love and say it over and over again and they'll create wild rhymes and nonsensical combinations of words. More than anything, they love authors who play with language—and no one does it better than Dr. Seuss, of course.

For reluctant writers, language has become merely functional—a painful means to an end. They have forgotten, or never knew, how close language is to song and play. Writing is not just about spelling rules and transitional sentences. In the nonsense rhymes of childhood, they can rediscover a joy in words.

THE ACTIVITY

1. Read a picture book that has some wonderful language in it—perhaps *Jonathan and His Mommy* by Irene Smalls, which is filled with great sounds and rhythms. As students listen to the story, ask them to write down any words they like the sounds of. They don't have to know what the words mean. They just have to like the way they sound.

2. Pass out dictionaries and let students browse through all the words. Let them look for words they like the sound of. Maybe these are words they know, maybe not. Have them make a list of at least ten words.

3. Now have them write a story that uses most or all of those words in some way. The story can be very simple—perhaps about a simple kids' activity like brushing teeth, bugging a sibling, or eating candy.

4. Students may now want to try inventing their own words, as Dr. Seuss does. They can make up four or five words and again try writing a simple story that uses them.

5. Still another way for students to play with the music of language is to take a story they have already written, copy it, and cut it up into individual words. Then they can have fun rearranging the order of words and sentences. All kinds of new rhythms and meanings will begin to emerge. More than anything, students begin to discover that they need not feel intimidated by language but can have fun with it instead.

Make-believe

Little kids don't bother separating the real from the make-believe. For them, anything can happen; thus picture books easily mix the fantastical and the ordinary, whether it is Max in *Where the Wild Things Are* being sent to bed without his dinner and taking a boat journey from his bedroom, or a toy gorilla coming to life on a little girl's birthday in Anthony Browne's *Gorilla*.

One of our greatest challenges as thinkers and writers is to remember just how many possibilities there always are. How many different ways can we look at a situation? How many different answers can we generate? How many different questions? The great thinkers and creators have never limited themselves to the possible, but have instead given their imaginations free rein.

THE ACTIVITY

1. Have students imagine that they are four or five again and ask them to think about their day and to make a list of "what if" questions. Encourage them to be as silly, wild, and outrageous as possible! In *Cloudy With a Chance of Meatballs*, for instance, there is land where it rains orange juice and pancakes for breakfast! What if the snowflakes turned to candy gumdrops when they fell? What if the kid sitting next to

me suddenly turned into a fox? What if my dog could talk?

2. Now ask students to think about an ordinary activity—a trip to the candy store, riding on the bus, playing in the backyard—and imagine something magical happening. Have them write about it in their notebooks.

3. Finally, ask students the question, "If absolutely anything could happen in your story, what would a three- to five-year-old want to have happen in it?" Encourage students to write a story in which anything goes, in which whatever they want to happen, can.

Storyboards

....

After students have written a number of stories, they will be ready to choose one to create a book with. I require that students plan how their books are going to look—how many pictures they will have (and of what), as well as roughly how many words will be on each page. In making these decisions, students must pay careful attention to their language and, quite naturally, they will be thinking about leads, paragraph breaks, and transitions.

Planning the layout for their picture books is often the activity that wins over the very last holdouts among the reluctant writers. Again and again, I have seen students who have barely written a single word up until then begin to create a story as they draw their pictures. The tangible joy of creating a physical object suddenly makes the actual writing seem real and worthwhile.

THE ACTIVITY

1. Students need to choose one story from among the many they have written to turn into a picture book. They may want to do this in groups, again sharing all that they have written. Some students may find they want to write another story.

2. Once students have settled on a particular story, I give them the storyboards, large sheets of paper with small blocks that represent the pages of their books.

Before they begin making their book, they need to know what pictures they will need to draw or create (perhaps using cutouts from magazines or photographs) and where they will place their words.

3. Studying the picture books in the classroom, students will discover that sometimes the words appear at the bottom of the page with the picture on top, while in other instances the words appear on one page and a picture on the other, and so forth. Before beginning their own storyboards, students may wish to consider all the options.

4. As students plan their storyboards, they should make sure to leave a space for copyright information, a dedication, and an author's biography.

5. Now students can take regular-size paper and begin creating the actual book, using their storyboard as a map of how to draw and design it.

Making a Book

Here's a simple technique for creating a picture book.

1. Stack sheets of $8^1/2$- by 14-inch paper, as much as you'll need to form the book, plus one extra page. Staple them together down the middle.

2. Place two $8^1/2$- by 7-inch pieces of cardboard on top of the sticky side of an 11- by 16-inch sheet of contact paper, leaving a small gap of about $1/8$-inch for the book's spine. Fold the contact paper around the edges of the cardboard. This is the book's cover.

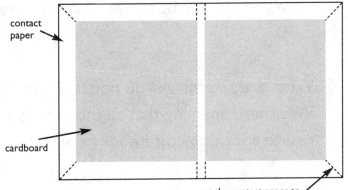

contact paper

cardboard

cut the contact paper to fold it over cardboard

3. With the cover open, glue the first page of the book down on the left side and the last page down on the right. Fit the middle of the book into the space for the book's spine. Allow to dry.

4. Fold the book in half and enjoy it!

Picture Book Response

Over the next _____ weeks we will be writing, illustrating, and making our own picture books. Today read at least four of the books in class. Remember: These are books written for little kids and you are reading them to get an idea of what kind of book you would like to create.

1. List the titles and authors of the four books that you read.

2. Which book did you like the most, and why?

3. Which book that you read do you think a three- to five-year-old would like the most, and why?

4. What are five things you notice about picture books that are different from the chapter books you may have read?

5. What are five things you notice about the writing in picture books? Was there anything that all the stories had in common, or that you realize a lot of picture books do?

6. When you were reading these stories, did they make you remember anything from when you were little or about other little kids that you know? What?

Prewriting Activity Sheet

1. Think of a boy or girl you know between the ages of three and six. Describe the child with as many specifics as you can. What does he or she look like? How does he or she act? What are some things he or she has done or said? How do you know this child?

2. Make a list of at least five completely ordinary things that happened to you when you were little but that felt like big events just because you'd never done them before or because you were so small. Some examples might be a trip to the zoo, a subway ride, a birthday party.

3. Make a list of at least five extraordinary things that happened to you when you were little. Some examples might be, "The time I got a fever of 104 degrees and was rushed to the hospital," or, "The time I got to be on television."

4. What were your favorite things when you were little? Food? Activities? People? Things? Places?

5. What kinds of things scared you when you were little?

6. Write about one of your earliest memories from childhood.

7. Write about any animals you had when you were little. Or, if you didn't have any animals, write about the kind of animals you loved or were interested in.

8. If you can remember, write about the kinds of daydreams and imaginings you used to have. Did you believe in magic? In superheroes? Did you want to be a pirate or a mermaid?

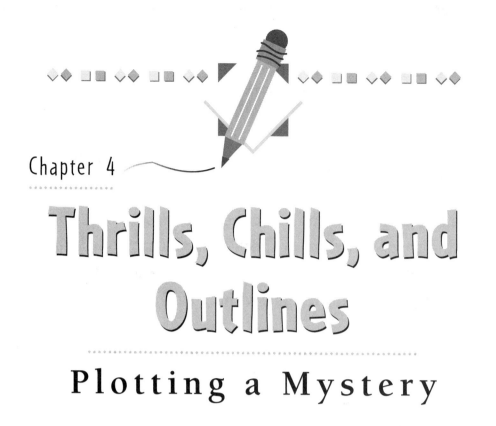

Chapter 4

Thrills, Chills, and Outlines

Plotting a Mystery

Many students read nothing but mysteries. They love the surprises, the suspenseful details, and, most of all, the challenge to figure out "who dunnit." They love imagining themselves as sleuths masterfully putting the pieces of the puzzle together. In a mystery, everything matters, everything could be a clue. Lurking in a casual description of the main character's room could be a crucial piece of evidence. Readers of mysteries know they can ignore nothing.

Writers of mysteries must also pay attention to details. Theirs is a deliberate kind of writing where nothing is left to chance. A good mystery is carefully plotted with each clue leading inexorably to the next, where the solution is at the same time surprising and inevitable. In many ways, the organizational strategies the mystery writer employs are little different than those of the essayist or research writer who builds the evidence towards a compelling thesis. Because of this, a genre study of mysteries provides the teacher with an opportunity to present outlining and sequencing skills many students find tedious. In addition, many of the artistic flourishes of good writing—the character development, the descriptions of settings—suddenly have an obvious purpose; they are concealing and revealing the clues to "who dunnit."

The Expert Witness

In the movie *My Cousin Vinnie*, in which a traveler through the South is wrongfully accused of murder, the crucial piece of evidence that proves the man's innocence comes from the lawyer's girlfriend. This woman knows more about cars than anybody. She can identify the treads of any tire, the kind of car that would have those treads, and she can show that it was not this man's car that was at the scene of the crime. As so often happens, the whole mystery hinges on expert testimony.

Mystery writers often rely on their knowledge of very specific subjects and environments. John Grisham, a Southern lawyer, writes about Southern law firms. P. D. James was originally a British magistrate; she knows the ins and outs of the English legal system. Some mystery writers, of course, are great researchers. Ellis Peters weaves together her extensive knowledge of both herbs and medieval monastic life in her compelling mystery series about Brother Cadfael.

"Write what you know" is advice that is given to all writers, but for the mystery writer it matters perhaps most of all. Only when the mystery hinges on accurate but precise knowledge can it really surprise us. Only then can the mystery writer always stay a few steps ahead of the reader. For reluctant writers, the first step in writing a mystery, then, is to help them honor the knowledge they actually have. Often, if these students haven't been successful in school they don't feel they possess anything worth knowing, but of course this is not true. We are all experts on our own lives.

THE ACTIVITY

1. Begin by having students brainstorm a list of things they know about better than anybody else. Encourage them to think beyond school to their lives, their interests, their hobbies. Maybe one student is a Civil War buff, another knows everything about a certain computer game or television show, still another is an avid basketball fan. For some students the list may even be as simple as "my dog, my bedroom, my grandfather." That is enough for any writer.

2. Now have the students pick one of the items from their list and write about what they know on this topic. What do they know about it that few other people know? What are the little tidbits of information that will come in handy when planting clues? Remind them that it is often the seemingly trivial details that are at the heart of successful mysteries.

3. Next, have students make a list of things that they would like to find out about. What are some real questions they have? These don't have to be academic, either. I wish I knew how a television really worked, I wish I knew more about when my grandmother was a little girl. . . .

4. Invite students to research one of those questions. How will they find out the answer? On the Internet, in a book, in an interview? Writing a mystery could even be the culmination of a research project. Perhaps students have been researching a particular historical period or scientific principle. The information they have found could be used as clues in their story.

5. Once students have laid out their knowledge, have them read it over and think about how it could be used in a mystery. Just as they are an expert on Beanie Babies, so will their detective be. The next question then is, "What kind of mystery will involve a Beanie Babies clue?"

What If . . . ?

How do we decide what to write about? At first, the beginning writer thinks that involves an act of pure imagination or, to a lesser degree, imitating something seen on television. An eleven-year-old girl I taught began her mystery in the police station with a grisly murder committed by a wronged boyfriend. "Have you ever been in a police station?" I asked. "No," was the answer. "Do you want to spend time in a police station or a morgue?" "No," again. Nor was this particular girl very interested in boyfriends yet.

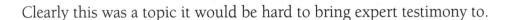

Clearly this was a topic it would be hard to bring expert testimony to.

When she began to look at her own life, however, she discovered that it was full of interesting possibilities for mysteries. There was the time her parents were two hours late picking her up at the airport. They said they were caught in traffic, but what were they really doing? Who was her father really talking to on the phone later that night? In time, she was writing compellingly about a girl, much like herself, investigating a strange intrigue that involved her parents.

The mystery writer looks at everyday events and asks, "What if. . .?" What if things are not what they seem?

THE ACTIVITY

1. There are secrets everywhere! Ask students to look around the room and imagine that nothing is what it appears to be. What if that girl I eat lunch with were really a child movie star in hiding? What if that sloppy painting were really a priceless masterpiece stolen by my teacher, an art thief? What if each day fish were mysteriously disappearing from the fish tank? Have students make a list of "what if" questions.

2. Now ask students to think about their daily lives and to ask the same "what if" questions. They may even want to do this for homework, noticing all the little details they can question as they move through their day. What if, as in *Scared Stiff* by Willo Davis Roberts, your mother never came home after work? Where might she be? What if, as in *Is Anybody There?* by Eve Bunting, you came home and noticed there was a missing piece of meatloaf? Who ate it if no one was home?

3. Once students have a number of these kinds of questions, they can begin to think about the mystery that they would like to write. They must be the villain and the detective all at once, thinking about both what the crime or mystery is and how it will be solved. As they begin to narrow in on their mystery, they should think about their earlier work on expert testimony. Does the mystery they imagined allow them to make use of some specialized knowledge or area that they would like to research?

Miss Scarlet and Colonel Mustard— Collecting Colorful Characters

Mysteries are peopled by complex, unpredictable individuals. No matter how ordinary they at first appear, they all turn out to have secrets, grudges, and lurking motives. Everyone in a mystery could be guilty. Again and again, in *Death on the Nile*, in *And Then There Were None*, in *Murder on the Orient Express*, the grand dame of mystery writing, Agatha Christie, assembled a hodgepodge of distinctive personalities and then set about describing how they behaved after the first dead body was found.

Making a character come to life on the page is always difficult, but it can also be one of the most enjoyable and exciting parts of writing. Like the Mr. Potato Head toy children love to play with, the bits and pieces of different people can be mixed and matched to create surprisingly interesting characters. In my mystery, about an old neighbor who suddenly disappears, the neighbor talks endlessly about his college days like an actual neighbor of mine did, but I want him to look like my great-uncle with his drooping eyes and drooping mustache. And I think too that he will have had a terrible fight with his only brother when he was younger, like my grandfather did. Maybe I will have him wear only silk bow ties like my friend's father. Before I know it, I have created strange old Mr. Swagglemere.

THE ACTIVITY

1. Cut out a lot of photographs of interesting-looking people of all ages. Make sure they are pictures of real people and not models. The newspapers, women's magazines, and *National Geographic* are good places to find such photos. Now invite the students to look at the pictures and choose one of them to be a character in their story.

2. As students look at their photo, tell them to imagine the whole story of this person. Encourage them to borrow details from the lives of other people they know—just like real writers do! Students should think about the character's nationality, upbringing, family life, education, friends, and, of course, secrets. What are this

person's hobbies, interests, aversions, passions? What is this person good at? What is this person bad at? What would you never know about this person just from looking at him or her? Have students write down all their answers.

Remind them, too, that they may not use all of this information in their actual story but that knowing it will change the way they write about this person. The more real and complete the character is for the writer, the more believable for the reader.

3. Have students take their new character and imagine how this person walks and talks. Students can actually pretend to be the character and the teacher can be a talk-show host introducing these new personalities to the class.

4. Finally, students will want to imagine as fully as they can all of the characters in their story. They may not necessarily need to repeat this entire activity for each new character, but at the very least they should write a description of what the person looks like and his or her history and secrets. The mystery writer, like the good detective, must know everything about everybody.

The Formula: Creating a Blueprint for a Mystery

There are two different stories in a mystery: the story of the events that have led up to the mystery, and the story of how the detective discovers clues and finally figures out what that first story is. The mystery writer knows the first story but writes the second.

A mystery begins *in medias res*, in the middle of things. Typically, in the opening the detective is pulling up to a crime scene. What happened and why? In a number of mysteries without actual crimes, the main character stumbles upon something out of the ordinary and realizes that there is more to the situation than meets the eye. What's really going on? The job then of the detective is to work backward, to follow the trail of clues back to the original cause of the whole mystery.

Along the way, the detective usually puts the clues together incorrectly. Some

things aren't even clues at all, just red herrings, evidence that distracts the detective from the real solution. But eventually, some crucial piece of evidence is uncovered that makes all the earlier clues fall into place and leads the detective to the right answer. The story ends back at the beginning, at the revelation of the event where all of the trouble started.

This is the blueprint or formula for a mystery. Of course, in more sophisticated stories there will be exceptions, but, as always, the exceptions prove the rule. For a reluctant writer, having such a framework for a story can be helpful. Knowing the whole story before beginning to write makes the project feel manageable. Instead of writing off into the unknown, they are having fun revealing and concealing clues. In addition, learning how to follow a particular formula in writing is important—since in the future students will face research papers and five-paragraph essays that will demand similar preplanning.

THE ACTIVITY

1. Begin by explaining the formula for a mystery and seeing how many students recognize it either from their reading or their television viewing. Some students may even be able to figure out what comes next.

   ### The Formula

   - An Inexplicable Event causes the detective to look for clues.
   - The Detective collects clues A, B, and C. (One of these clues isn't even a clue and has nothing to do with the solution at all. It is a red herring.)
   - The Detective arrives at Solution 1.
   - Clue D turns up, however, and doesn't fit with Solution 1.
   - The Detective collects clues E and F, but something seems to be missing.
   - Clue G turns up and the whole puzzle fits together, and the Detective produces Solution 2, the Answer.

   Explain to students that there may be more or fewer clues and more than one inaccurate solution. In addition, usually the clues pull the detective back in time to the beginning of the story. The first clues are the most recent, the later clues happened closer to the cause of the whole mystery.

2. In order for students to write blueprints for their own mysteries, they must first decide two things: They must know what the cause of the mystery is and what will be the Inexplicable Event. That is, they must know the beginning and the ending of the first story, the story that the detective will slowly discover.

3. They must also then decide what will be the Clues, both accurate and false, that they will have the Detective find. In order to come up with Clues, they can return to the events leading up to the Inexplicable Event and think about what evidence resulting from certain actions and decisions of the characters might have been left behind.

4. Have students use the A Blueprint for a Mystery activity sheet (page 50) to plan out their mysteries. Part I is the first story and what they must know to begin writing. Part II is the second story and the one they actually tell.

5. After students have a clear plan for their mysteries, they should begin to write.

Hidden in Plain Sight: Using Details and Descriptions

In the midst of a description of what is on a character's desk, the writer mentions a letter with a foreign postmark. But as the writer has also detailed strange books, old cups with half-drunk coffee, a sharp letter opener, and an odd Egyptian amulet, the reader pays little attention to it. Only later, when the detective produces it as a piece of crucial evidence, will we even remember that it was there.

Good clues are there for the reader to notice, but in a suspenseful mystery it can be hard to tell what is real evidence and what is not. Only the detective with his or her superior skills of discrimination knows just what's important. The most satisfying mystery is one in which we feel that if we had just been paying more careful attention earlier on we, too, could have figured it out. In *The Face on the Milk Carton*, the main character, Janie, has a dream toward the beginning of the story that turns out much later to be an important clue.

Reluctant writers want to get to the point and get the writing over with. "Why bother with all this meaningless detail?" they'll often ask. But in a mystery, detail and description serve an obvious purpose—to simultaneously reveal and conceal the clues. If the mystery writer gets to the point too fast, there is no suspense and no mystery at all.

THE ACTIVITY

1. Place a number of different items—interesting objects, letters, books, etc.—on a table like a still life. Make sure one of the items has a seemingly insignificant feature—a crack in a vase, a penny from 1932. This, of course, is the clue, and you will have it written down on a piece of paper you have put away.

2. Now invite the students to write a description of the still life, noticing as many details as they can. When they are done, they should share aloud what they have written. Did any of them notice the clue? Were any of them successful detectives? If not, send them back to try again!

3. Explain to students that if there had been only the penny on the table, it would have been easy to recognize it as evidence, but because it was combined with so much else it remained hidden to all but the most observant eyes. When they write their own mystery novels, they will continually be setting up just such scenes where there is a lot to look at but only one thing that matters.

4. Finally, have them choose a clue from their mysteries and write about it in such a way that it is present in the description but not obvious. To test their success, they can share their descriptions with each other. If the reader guesses the clue too effortlessly, that means they need to embed it in more descriptive writing.

5. As students follow their blueprints writing their mysteries, keep reminding them to take their time and linger on the details and descriptions that build suspense.

One Dark and Stormy Night–A Mystery Reading

In a classic mystery, the detective assembles all the suspects in the drawing room and slowly reveals each of their motives and opportunities, slowly narrowing in on the villain. To celebrate finishing their mystery stories, it can be fun to reenact just such a scene. Darken the room, put chairs in a circle, light candles, and hang cobwebs. Invite family and friends. If you have never done a reading with your students, it may be important to go over the following procedures.

THE ACTIVITY

1. Make sure that all the students have practiced reading aloud their stories. The more often they have done so, the easier it will be to read with inflection, to look up from the paper, to give the different characters different voices. They may want to type and double-space their mysteries to make them easy to read.

2. Students may discover, too, that in preparing for their reading they want to make changes to their text. This happens to all writers and is one of the reasons they like to share their work out loud.

3. Prepare the listeners by reminding them what kind of audience they would like to have—attentive, quiet, thoughtful. It can help them focus, too, if they have something they are listening for. Ask them to let the writer know what character they most enjoyed or what was the most interesting clue or most suspenseful piece of description and why. If there is time, pause after each reading and have the listeners write a note to the writer about the piece. The writer then gets very immediate feedback.

4. After a reading, it can also be productive to provide the writers with time to go back and look over their pieces. Writing is a process, and often it is just when we think we are done we come up with the idea we wish we had had all along. After hearing their classmates' work, reluctant writers in particular may want to have another chance.

A Blueprint for a Mystery

I. The Story Behind the Mystery:

    A. Original Event (cause of all the trouble):

    B. Subsequent Events

        1.

        2.

        3

        4.

    C. Inexplicable Event

II. Uncovering the Mystery

    A. The Inexplicable Event:

        1. Clues

            a.

            b.

            c.

        2. Red Herrings

            a.

            b

            c.

    B. Solution 1: The Wrong Answer

    C. New Evidence

        1. Clues

            a.

            b.

        2. The Missing Piece of the Puzzle (the cause of everything)

    D. Solution 2: The Explanation of the Mystery

Chapter 5

Sportswriting

The Voice of Authority

The more knowledgeable and passionate we are about a subject, the easier it is to write about. For many students, what they care about most is sports. They know statistics and histories; they can provide detailed accounts of games; they have considered opinions on draft picks, coaches, the best players, and why their team is or isn't winning. Often, however, in the writing-workshop classroom, the imperative to "write what you know" is misinterpreted to mean "write about yourself." Yet, as the greatest writers realize, we need not reveal the intimate details of our own lives in order to write emotionally and well.

The challenge to write convincingly about the drama and action of sports has again and again been met by serious writers. Fishing and bullfighting fascinated Hemingway, and Joyce Carol Oates and Norman Mailer have both written remarkably well about boxing. And then there are the legions of columnists and reporters who each day in their local newspapers help us experience the game as if we were there.

Kids who don't seem to read at all nevertheless read the sports pages and pore over *Sports Illustrated* every week. They may not be paying much attention to who is writing these articles or what techniques they employ to capture the action of the event, but they are often very familiar with the genre. At least unconsciously, they have learned how a sports piece is supposed to sound, how it begins and ends, and what kinds of details it includes. Within the classroom, then, the task is to make students aware of that knowledge and put it to use writing their own pieces and then creating their own sports magazine.

The Sportswriter's Beat

Most sportswriters have a particular sport they report on. Sometimes they even have a particular team they follow. Often, TV commentators are actually ex-players with an inside take on what's really going on. Either way, the reporters have a beat, a focus for their research and writing.

What's important when students are writing about sports is that they, too, develop an area of expertise, a beat. It may arise from a sport they are already involved or interested in, or it may be something new they come to learn about and appreciate. For their writing, however, they should be covering sports they can actually watch in real life. The sportswriter's job is to make us feel as if we were there, and to that end the writer must see the event as it happens.

THE ACTIVITY

1. In groups or as a class, students should brainstorm a list of all the different sporting events that are happening in and around their community. They should consider sports that are being played by their peers in and around school—the soccer and baseball leagues, the gymnastics and swim teams—and sports that are played by professionals or high school students that they might have access to. Perhaps a minor league baseball team practices in their town, or they could attend practices and games for the high school football team. They should also remember to include nonteam sports—local marathons, cycling races, or horse shows.

   It's also possible for the class to choose as their beat the school's gym class. The phys. ed. teacher could be involved in talking about the sport the class is playing, and it would be very easy for the students to attend events.

2. Next students should decide on a beat. They should choose a sport they can actually watch and which they know something about or have some interest in. They shouldn't choose a sport they are a player in unless they can watch other teams

competing. It's very hard to write about a game when you are trying to win it.

3. Finally, students can begin to become familiar with a professional reporter's beat. Either in the local newspaper or in *Sports Illustrated* or *Field and Stream*, they should read about their favorite sport and begin to notice who is doing the writing. They can cut out these articles and keep them in a folder. As they reread them, they can underline sentences or words the writer used that they like. Some students may even begin to notice that certain writers have a particular way of writing, a voice that they can recognize even when it doesn't say who wrote the article.

Describing the Event—You Were There!

No one on the PGA tour is like Tiger. The hole is a par 5, which means an average player will likely need at least five tries to get the ball 485 yards from tee to hole. Tiger's first shot was a monstrous drive, so long that his second shot required a mere 8-iron, which put him on the green. Now he is about to hit shot number three. As he considers it, thousands of people are considering him. They are lining the green and the fairway, and what distinguishes them most is how motionless they remain as he draws the putter back and brings it forward against the ball. Only when the ball begins to roll do they dare move, and only when it closes in on the hole do they begin to make noise, and only when it drops into the cup do they begin to roar. "Let the record show that on Friday, April 11, at 5:31 P.M. Eastern Daylight Time, Tiger Woods takes his first lead ever at the Masters."

from "Golf's Saving Grace," by David Finkel, for the *Washington Post Magazine*

In the days of radio, the reporter would rapidly describe each moment of a game as it was happening so that the listeners at home could feel just like they were in the stadium. Today, with live coverage on television, reporters tend to analyze the event—what's good about it, what a certain player's weaknesses are, what's likely to happen in the future. The newspaper or magazine reporter tends to do both—share opinions and make

predictions, but most of all to let us relive each delicious moment of the game.

To that end, the sportswriter has to have a keen eye for both the big plays and the significant details—the moment when the tennis player aces his opponent and the moment when the skater glances over at her coach just before gliding off across the ice.

THE ACTIVITY

1. Divide the class into groups and explain that two members in the group will engage in either an arm-wrestling match or a round of paper football. The students who are not playing will watch the event, take notes on it, and then write a description of what happened.

2. Some students will find that taking notes is helpful. Others will prefer to watch very carefully, making sure they don't miss anything, and then write when they are done.

3. When students have all finished one description of an event, the class can share their writing and talk about the kinds of details that give a sense of what was actually happening. Some students may have noticed the expressions on the players' faces, others may have noticed what they said, and still others may have written about the onlookers or the setting for the competition.

4. After sharing their first descriptions, students should try the exercise again, this time paying even more attention to the details of the event. Remind students to use all their senses, to note not just what they see but what they hear and feel, as well.

5. If possible, for homework, students should try writing a description of an event from their beat—a practice or even a game. What kinds of details will give the reader the experience of having been there?

Active Language

Oakland had a runner at first and one out in the fifth, with the Yankees leading by 3-0, when A.J. Hinch slugged a long drive to deep center. Bernie Williams got a good jump on the ball, but it still appeared as if the ball had gone over his head—until he reached up with his glove hand, on a dead run, and speared the ball.

from *The New York Times*, April 8, 1999

The hardest thing to capture in sportswriting is the speed, the exertion, the sheer energy of the game itself. Because of this, sportswriters rely on action verbs. What did the player do? He *leapt*, he *slammed*, he *catapulted* through the air. The language of sportswriting tends to be lean, with no excess adjectives and adverbs. The power of the writing is in the verbs.

THE ACTIVITY ◇◆ ◇◆ ◇◆ ◇◆ ◇◆ ◇◆ ◇◆ ◇◆

1. Have students think of their favorite sport and make a list of all the verbs they can think of that apply to it. (For example, with baseball they might have *slugged*, *hit*, *struck out*, *slid*, etc.)

2. Now have students use a thesaurus to expand their lists. If they are not sure how to use one, show them how to look up one of their verbs and find other action words that are similar to it and that they think sound appropriate. When they are done, they can share their lists and note any words of their peers that they especially like. Explain to them that they are not limited to any single set of words. In the passage above, for instance, Bernie Williams is described as "spearing" the ball. He didn't actually use a spear, of course, but that word gives us a clear image of the directness and ferocity with which he moved his body and arm.

3. One interesting exercise is to have students take an article from the sports section describing an event and to black out with a marker all the words except the verbs. Then they can read it aloud and hear how it sounds. "Leading, slugged, appeared, speared." The vitality of the piece is often in those words.

4. Then, either in class or for homework, students can write another description of a sporting event, this time focusing on the verbs. When they are done with their pieces, they should try reading them to each other with all words but the verbs left out. Again, how does it sound? Is it "ran, stopped, went, did" or "flew, skidded, leapt, dunked"?

Fact vs. Opinion

MacInnis's slapper, which typically travels at more than 90 mph, remains the fastest and most fearsome in the game, but it's his broad range of skills that makes him SI's [Sports Illustrated's] choice for the Norris Trophy. At week's end MacInnis led all defensemen with 19 goals and 49 points. He was playing a staggering 28 minutes and 51 seconds per game, and his plus-26 rating, tops by far on the Blues, was seventh-best in the league.

from "Mr. Everything," by Kostya Kennedy, for *Sports Illustrated*

Students can argue for hours over why this team is better or why that gymnast should have received a higher score. They back up their opinions with statistics and stories and lots of interesting facts. When they are asked to write an essay, however, they are often at a loss as to how to structure a winning argument. In order to do so, they need to be clear about the difference between facts and opinions and how to use one to support the other.

THE ACTIVITY

1. Ask students to write down what they think is the best brand of ice cream. When they are done, list all the answers on the board and then invite them to convince their classmates of their choice. Some will say that this brand has more flavors or uses no artificial ingredients. Others will note that the one tastes better or is sweeter. Write all their reasons on the board as well.

2. Now invite them to think about which justifications are facts and which are opinions. Explain to them that there is no disagreement about a fact—one can present

evidence to prove it—whereas an opinion cannot be proved. That this brand uses no artificial ingredients is clear from checking the label. That this one tastes better is entirely subjective. Go through the entire list on the board, discussing which reasons are facts and which are opinions.

3. When students feel confident about the difference between facts and opinions, invite them to think of a strong opinion they have about a team or a sports figure. Who is the best quarterback? Why do the Bulls always win? Who should be nominated to the Hall of Fame? After they form an opinion, they can make a list of all the facts they have to support it, being careful not to support one opinion with another.

4. Have students read some of the editorials in the sports pages and notice how the writers support their opinions. What kinds of information do they draw on? How do they present it? What makes their arguments most convincing?

The Magic Moment

Chris Childs spit a tooth into his hand and fixed a menacing stare on Dikembe Mutombo, who trotted away innocently. It was all Childs could do not to dart toward the Hawks' towering collection of pointy elbows and bony kneecaps and start swinging away without regard to Mutombo's yard-long reach advantage.

He'll save the retaliation for another game. It was too important for him to keep his cool and stay in a game that had a desperate, do-or-die feel to it.

"Childs Takes It On the Chin, But Knicks Hold On,"
by Selena Roberts for *The New York Times*, 4/10/99

The best sports events seem to have one: the moment that seems to make or break the competition, the moment chosen for instant replay, the moment after which nothing is the same. Part of being a great sportswriter is knowing how to recognize that moment

and capture its full intensity and meaning with words. In a certain sense, the writer even has a hand in creating that moment by drawing our attention to it, showing us what to notice and where to look.

THE ACTIVITY

1. Start with a class discussion about everyone's favorite moments from a sports event. Encourage students to describe the moment and to explain why they think it was so memorable or important to them or to the game.

2. Now the class should attend a live sporting event together—a local baseball game, a gym class, or some other sport the class can do themselves with one half watching and the other playing. Tell students to watch carefully, writing down details they want to remember for their writing. When the game is over, students should ask themselves, "What was the most important moment in that game and why?" By answering that question, they begin to make meaning of the event, not only to describe it for the reader but to explain it as well.

3. Have students write about the magic moment of the game. How can they best capture it? What kinds of information will the reader need in order to understand how important it was? What other details from the game will have to be included? What quotes from the players might add additional support to their writing?

The Interview

Asked if this would be the first of many Williams sisters championship jousts, Venus Williams said: "Exactly. The new era has arrived for women's tennis. We've come a long way but this is what we always thought we would do."

from "First It's Williams and Then Williams,"
by Robin Finn, for *The New York Times*

The reporter rushes to the locker room or pulls the skater aside as she glides off the ice. What was it like out there? What were you thinking about when you landed that triple lutz? How did you feel? Watching the game, there is only so much we can know. We know what they did, but not why. We know what happened, but not how it felt. The only way to answer those questions is to talk to the players themselves.

Most students imagine that for interviews they need to write out a list of questions and then diligently ask them, recording the answers. The sportswriter, however, must respond spontaneously to circumstances just after they have happened. The sportswriter may know the game well and the players' histories, but, finally, the only real preparation is the game itself.

THE ACTIVITY ◇◆ ◇◆ ◇◆ ◇◆ ◇◆ ◇◆ ◇◆ ◇◆

1. Bring in a videotape of a sporting event and have the students watch it together and write down any questions they might have for the players. What would they like to know? What might other people like to know?

2. Students should share questions and think about the kinds of things they might ask the participants of an event. Explain to students that they are trying to get the athletes to say interesting things, and because of that they need to ask questions that will get that person talking, questions that call for more than a yes or no answer.

3. Let students role-play some practice interviews. One student can pretend to be a participant from the event watched on the video, and the other can be the interviewer. The other students can watch and write down the questions and follow-up questions they would have asked. Then another pair can role-play an interview. Given students' level of expertise and confidence, this may be enough, or you may want to break them into smaller groups to practice more interviews.

4. After the interview, the sportswriter needs to decide what are the gems amid all the rocks of the interviewee's words. In most articles there are only one or two quotes from the players. Which one or two would the interviewers from class choose to use and why? What did the participant say that was surprising, outra-

geous, or just fascinating? It may be helpful at this point to read some articles from the sports pages and to note the kind of quotes the writers are using.

5. The final challenge is for students to try to conduct a real interview at a real event. They should be prepared with notebook and pen, or even a tape recorder, if possible. Students may want to share their complete interviews together in groups and then help each other pull out the two or three best quotes for their articles.

The Lead

For a man considered to be baseball's bastion of truth and integrity, Mark McGwire is one hell of a liar. "Nothing at all," was his reply to the simple somewhat silly question, What about this year's spring training is different from last year's? "It's the same as always." This was roughly 30 seconds after McGwire, en route to the visitors' club-house at Dodgertown in Vero Beach, Fla., was greeted by a throng of 100 or more fans—including one woman who'd waited six hours for an autograph—pushing and shoving one another against a metal fence. Nothing at all?

"Still Jackin," by Jeff Pearlman, for *Sports Illustrated*

Writers have to work hard to catch their readers' attention, making sure they will be hooked right from the beginning. They don't begin their pieces dutifully with, "At spring training last Thursday in Florida there were predictably a lot of fans outside the gate waiting for Mark McGwire." Instead, writers startle us or ask us a question; they pull us in, make us want to know what the whole story really is.

THE ACTIVITY

1. Begin by having students read over the first sentences and paragraphs of a lot of different sports articles. Which ones catch their attention, and why? What kinds of information or details do the writers lead off with?

2. Have students look over their notes and descriptions and interview material and write five different leads for their article about a sporting event. Have them try starting a lead with a quote, with an important moment or detail from the game, with a question or their own creative idea.

3. As they work on their leads, encourage students to think about the word *lead*. A leader takes us somewhere, guides us to a particular destination. Where are they going in their article? What do they ultimately want to say about the game? What is the big opinion they have about it (their thesis) that they want to share? The lead should get us started in that direction.

4. Sometimes it can be fun for students to imagine the lead as the first step of a stone path, or the first rung of a ladder, and to actually draw the empty circles or rungs on a sheet of paper. If the lead is first, what will come second, third, and fourth? Where will we end up at the end of the writing? This is a very concrete way of out-lining the piece. Interestingly, the lead itself can often determine where the piece will go and what it will be about.

The Four W's—A Journalist's Concern

Who? What? When? and Where? This is the information that any journalist must pro-vide for the reader—the names, dates, places, and other significant facts. A journalist cannot assume that the reader has any prior knowledge about the subject at hand; it's his or her job to provide whatever information the readers need in order to make sense of the piece.

But a journalist is also a writer and doesn't just hurl those facts at the reader in a big, indigestible lump. The challenge is to sneak that information in artfully—to provide it in such a way that the reader learns it but does not lose the thread of the story. For this reason, inexperienced writers often do better to fill in this information after they have fin-ished a piece and have developed an angle on their story, going back and clarifying and making additions where necessary.

THE ACTIVITY

1. Write the following sentence on the board: *This person did this thing there at that time.* What questions do students have? They are sure to ask who, what, where, and when.

2. Now have students read one another's pieces in groups and make note of any places where factual information or background material seems to be missing. Using different-ent colored pens, they can write their "W" questions in the margins of the writer's piece. Names, dates, locations—this is what they should look for.

3. Explain to students that now they are going to learn a sneak play in writing called **the appositive phrase**—a way of sliding in necessary information without interrupting the flow of the story. An example:

   Mike Keane, a former Ranger, opened the scoring at even strength against Dan Cloutier, the backup goalie, who played well while stopping 31 of 34 shots.

   The appositive phrase modifies the noun preceding it and is usually set apart by commas. This is a very useful way of including facts and background material.

4. Now, using the feedback from their group editing session, along with their new sneak play, have students revise their pieces, adding any necessary clarifying information.

The Sports Section

In addition to having students write individual pieces about sporting events, it can be exciting and worthwhile to have them actually produce a sports magazine or newspaper. When students' writing is intended for a real audience, it changes—it becomes more important to get it right, to get it good, to make it perfect.

The more real that magazine or newsletter, the more powerful an influence it will have on the students' writing process. If the students are just writing about games they have all seen on television, the writing obviously doesn't matter so much. If, however, they are covering local sporting events, then their writing will feel more current and relevant.

THE ACTIVITY   ◇◆ ◇◆ ◇◆ ◇◆ ◇◆ ◇◆ ◇◆ ◇◆

1. At this point, everyone in the class is a contributing editor, making decisions about how the magazine will look and contributing material for it. And the first choice the editorial staff has to make is who the audience for this work will be and what kind of topics and subjects will be covered. Are they going to offer their publication to other sixth graders? to the whole school? to a different school? Are they going to produce it online and make it available to students around the country?

   The answers to these questions will be determined by what kind of sporting events the class has access to write about. If they are only writing about the gym program, for instance, it may be better to distribute it only within the school.

2. Together, too, the staff must decide how many issues to offer—one or two, weekly or monthly, etc. The class needs to think about how quickly they can write and produce their magazine. An advantage to producing more than one issue is that students will be able to focus, the second time through, more on the quality of their writing and less on the logistics of getting the issue to press.

3. Depending on the technology available to the class, the magazine can be done completely on the computer, using a desktop publishing program, or could even be produced online. Of course, collating and copying everyone's essays and distributing the packet throughout the school is an exciting culmination to the unit.

A Last Word About Reluctance—Persistence

Nothing I did in my writing class worked for Eddie. He just hated it. At the beginning of the year, I had had many students who dreaded writing, but after lots of time playing in our notebooks, writing children's books and sports pages together, I had a group of motivated writers. But not Eddie. In March he was still sighing when he walked through the door and refusing to revise or even talk about anything.

Hard to write
Hard to phrase
Hard to read
Hard to understand
I'd rather be skiing
I'd rather be fishing
I'd rather be walking
I'd rather be talking
I'd rather be dead
Than alive writing
phrasing
reading
understanding
a poem

I had planned to do a unit on poetry with my class that spring, and I could well imagine what *that* was going to do to Eddie. It would send him over the edge, I was sure.

On the first day of our poetry unit, however, he brought me a poem (at right), a manifesto of sorts. I was stunned. What a wonderful piece of writing it was—passionate, direct, funny. It was the first time I'd ever seen him write about anything with any real feeling. I asked him if I could share it with the class. He was surprised, but he let me. And that began Eddie's career as a writer.

At last Eddie realized that he had something to say. He threw himself into our poetry unit, producing vibrant, startling pieces about skiing, the mountains, flying. He wrote and rewrote a memoir about fishing with his father, carefully thinking about each word, getting it just right. At the end of the year he wrote me:

"I feel that I have become a writer this year. I write what I see, what I feel, or what happens to me, or to anyone else for that matter. Before this year the only writing I did was on reports or tests. Now I can write stories where I hit the game-winning home run in the World Series or invent a cure for AIDS and become a world hero. In fact, I can make them happen in the same story."

To write well is to dare to speak with our own voice, and what triggers that breakthrough for different students can often be quite mysterious. I would never have thought poetry would work for Eddie (and certainly Eddie hadn't thought so either), but it did. So we can make our classrooms safe, try lots of different activities and genres, but most of all we must be persistent. We all have our own voice and, if we find it, we can all be writers.